I DON'T CHASE, I ATTRACT

HOW TO USE THE LAW OF ATTRACTION
TO BECOME A POWERFUL MANIFESTOR

VERA WRIGHT

Copyright ©2021 Vera Wright

All rights reserved.

ISBN: 9798490258797

To my dear husband, Bob.

Thanks for being living proof that manifesting true love is possible.

CONTENTS

	Introduction	7
Chapter 1	What Is The Law Of Attraction	13
Chapter 2	The Principles Of The Law Of Attraction	19
Chapter 3	How To Use The Law Of Attraction Effectively	25
Chapter 4	How To Use The Law Of Attraction For Specific Goals	31
Chapter 5	The Impact Of The Law Of Attraction	35
Chapter 6	Tips To Make The Law Of Attraction Work For You	39
Chapter 7	Using The Law Of Attraction To Create A Stress-Free Life	43
Chapter 8	The Power Of Positive Thinking	51
Chapter 9	7 Mindful Habits For Creating Positive Thoughts	57
Chapter 10	Manifestation And The Law Of Attraction	71
Chapter 11	How To Manifest Anything In 5 Steps	81
Chapter 12	The 5 Principles Of Manifestation	117
Chapter 13	7 Law Of Attraction Tips To Manifest Success	99
Chapter 14	Understanding Your Subconscious Mind	105
	Conclusion	111
	About The Author	113

INTRODUCTION

THERE ARE TWO DIFFERENT MINDSETS we can choose to have as we navigate this the world.

We are either chasing or attracting.

Many believe chasing and attracting are the same thing. Both involve getting the opportunities, people, dreams, and everything we want and believe we deserve. And on the surface, they may appear similar. But they are very different states, and they produce very different results.

Chasing seems to empower, but it's actually a depowering state. It shoots us down into a lower frequency—our chasing state is lined with desperation. We tie our worth to what we're chasing, and if we don't get what we're going after, we believe we have less worth. So we basically give our power to whatever or whoever we're chasing. By chasing, we are losing our sense of self. Whenever we lose our sense of self, we are watered down and not living our full potential. And this state doesn't attract anything. It becomes the opposite. We become a flipped magnet.

Now, remember, not chasing doesn't mean to stop being ambitious or not going after your dreams. I'm talking about a mindset, an intention, energy, where we pull from.

Attracting is a powerfilled state. You are focusing on improving over wanting. You are not exchanging who you are for what you want. You are not seeking approval and validation. You are not taking. You are giving by being the best version of yourself. And by being in this state, having this mindset, you are raising your vibration, living on a higher frequency, and attracting who and what you are meant to attract.

Attracting doesn't always mean looking for shiny things like clothes and money because shiny things won't take you to the next level. Attracting means getting things that line up with your purpose, that position you to head into the direction you were meant to, where you will be the boldest and brightest you've ever been.

I DON'T CHASE, I ATTRACT

Ever notice that when you're feeling crappy, the whole world seems hostile and unfair? ("That guy cut me off! Screw him!") But when you're in a good mood, the whole world appears friendly and appealing, and nothing can bring you down? ("Sure, go ahead, you must be in a hurry!")

Here's the truth: The world is no different in those days. You are different.

It all comes down to something called the Law of Attraction. The Law simply says: "What we think about, we bring about." It's the idea that we can attract anything we want into our lives by visualizing our desired results, using affirmations, expecting good things to happen, being appreciative, and taking inspired action.

This book was created to help you master the Law of Attraction and create a life you love. Each technique, step, and note in this book is here for you to practice and use it to your benefit. The more you practice positive thinking and use it for the Law of Attraction, the better your life will be. You will be more enriched, more fulfilled, and lead a better quality of life in general. This book will help you learn everything you need to become a Law of Attraction guru in your own life.

Through this book, you will learn how to start making

positive changes in your daily life and your life as a whole. You will learn to incorporate manifesting techniques into your daily practice so you can continue attracting your desired results and create the life you always wanted.

You will also learn why it is so important to practice gratitude and positive thinking every day, for these are two of the essential ingredients for manifesting your dream life.

Chapter One
WHAT IS THE LAW OF ATTRACTION?

ACCORDING TO QUANTUM PHYSICS, our thoughts have a frequency and a corresponding unique vibration that attracts similar frequencies into our lives. So negative thinking attracts negative energy; positive thinking attracts positive energy.

This also applies to group thinking or collective consciousness. When a collection of people together guide their mental energy for a positive outcome, the likelihood of their success is usually a lot higher than otherwise. Their collective power attracts positivity or negativity.

Lao Tzu, an ancient Chinese philosopher, once said: "Watch your thoughts, they become your words; watch your words, they become your actions; watch your actions, they become your habits; watch your habits, they become your character; watch your character, it becomes your destiny."

The idea that we attract what we put out has been around since ancient times, and many credit Buddha with first introducing this notion to the world.

THE 7 LAWS OF ATTRACTION

The Law of Attraction can be broken down into seven "mini-laws" that affect how the world responds to you and your lifechoces.

1. THE LAW OF MANIFESTATION

This is what most people think of when they hear the words "Law of Attraction." The Law of Manifestation states that our thoughts and feelings create our reality —and what we focus on is what we will manifest in our lives.

I DON'T CHASE, I ATTRACT

Law of Attraction affirmations are a powerful way to keep your goals top of mind and help you focus on what you want—as opposed to what you don't wish to—so you're able to create the life you desire.

2. THE LAW OF MAGNETISM

The Law of Magnetism states that everything that has happened in your life—the people, things, and opportunities that have come into your life, as well as the circumstances in which you have found yourself—is a result of the energy you put out into the world.

You attract what you are.

3. THE LAW OF UNWAVERING DESIRE

Do you genuinely want the things you believe you want?

The Law of Unwavering Desire states that your desire to achieve or attract a sure thing must be solid and unyielding for you to manifest it in your life. When your desires are weak, and without a rock-solid foundation, they won't be able to attract what you want.

4. THE LAW OF DELICATE BALANCE

The Universe is comprised of balance—between various

forces and elements. And as we are microcosms of the Universe, we also crave balance. When the different aspects of your life are in harmony, you can experience true peace and joy. But to achieve balance, appreciation and gratitude are required.

5. THE LAW OF HARMONY

The Law of Harmony describes the coordinated interplay of forces and elements that comprise the Universe. Harmony is the flow of life. When you are in tune with it, everything seems easy, as if you are swimming with the current rather than against it.

Tapping into the Law of Harmony and striving to live harmoniously with all other beings will open you to everything good that the Universe has to offer.

6. THE LAW OF RIGHT ACTION

The Law of Right Action states that your words and actions affect the world around you and determine the quality of your experiences in life. How you behave and treat others will determine how others treat you.

When you focus on the right action and are kind to others, always being sure to do what you wish done to them, you will attract more positivity into your life.

7. THE LAW OF UNIVERSAL INFLUENCE

It's easy to feel small and insignificant when staring up at the stars at night. But the truth is, every one of us is an integral part of the Universe. We make an impact on the world with everything we think and do. Our energy vibrations become a part of the fabric of the Universe.

That's why it's so crucial for you to be aware of your thoughts, feelings, and actions, as well as signs from the Universe, to demonstrate the impact of your efforts and point you in the direction of your dreams.

By doing so, you will effectively control your energy and increase the positive impact on the world around you.

Chapter Two

THE PRINCIPLES OF THE LAW OF ATTRACTION

NOW YOU KNOW THAT the Law of Attraction is a powerful force in the Universe that is already working. However, you may not be tapped into it so that it can benefit your life. The Law of Attraction tells us that we attract what we put out into the world. Still, you must understand and use its critical principles if you want this Law of the Universe to work for you.

1. LIKE ATTRACTS LIKE

The Universe is filled with matter that contains energy. This energy causes vibrations, and when objects or people have the same waves, they are drawn to each other. Matter attracts whatever is on its same wavelength.

Our feelings cause us to vibrate differently, so when you are experiencing an emotion, others who feel similarly will be drawn to you.

Our thoughts can control our feelings, too. So, negative thoughts lead to negative feelings, which lead to adverse actions, leading to negative people being attracted to us—misery loves company!

The same is true for positive emotions and thoughts.

2. YOUR MINDSET CONTROLS EVERYTHING ELSE

Having a positive outlook affects your emotions, choices, how you see the world, perceive others and their actions. The same is true for a negative mindset. This means that if you want to attract your dreams and bring more positive outcomes into your life, you must start with your attitude. Learning to think positively is crucial for attracting whatever you want in your life.

3. YOU HAVE THE POWER TO CHANGE YOUR LIFE

The Law of Attraction is at work all the time, whether you choose to take advantage of it or not. When you decide that you are ready to create your reality deliberately and intentionally, you can start to harness this power to accomplish whatever you set out to do in your life.

4. YOU MUST CONCEPTUALIZE AND ASK FOR WHAT YOU WANT

For the Law of Attraction to work, the Universe needs to know what you most desire. This requires you to imagine what you want in as much detail as possible. Creating a mental or physical picture of your goal is helpful.

What is most important is that you imagine how accomplishing this goal will make you feel. What will it mean for your goals and values? Why is this important to you? This visualization can help guide your work toward manifesting your reality.

5. ALL YOUR CHOICES HAVE CONSEQUENCES.

The Law of Attraction is founded on the principles of cause and effect, that all actions react somewhere and at some time. Because of this, every choice you make, every emotion you express, every reaction you have to another person or life circumstance influences your life.

This means that you need to focus all your effort on making every choice, action, and response as positive as possible if you want the Law of Attraction to work favorably for you. Every decision matters; every step counts.

6. GIVING IS CRUCIAL

According to the Law of Attraction, if you want the Universe to provide for you, then you must be willing to give as well. The more you are ready to offer, the more you are likely to receive. Those who give to benefit others send out positive vibrations that help guide the Universe to them.

When you give, your mindset is open to receiving, enabling you to accept the gifts and opportunities provided to you.

* * *

I DON'T CHASE, I ATTRACT

WHAT THE LAW OF ATTRACTION ISN'T

Of course, positive thinking and belief alone won't make your dreams come true. You need to put in the work, too!

This means being congruent and living in alignment with your goals and taking the necessary steps to bring them to life.

For example, if your goal is to run a marathon in under four hours, you still need to put in the training and treat your body right in the months leading up to the race. From there, layering on some positive mantras and visualizations can further reinforce aligning your goal with the Universe.

Anyone prone to worry should also know that the Law of Attraction isn't a punishment. When some people first learn and start to practice this Law, sometimes they feel anxious that if they have bad thoughts or low vibrations, they can somehow mess up their life. Nobody is perfect, and we can use the law as a mirror of our mindset and self-worth when we're working through a challenging phase.

And always remember that at a certain point in manifestation, it's important to surrender and let the Universe take the wheel. Opportunities, people, and resources can show up out of the blue, so be open to them! Also, things may not play out exactly how you imagined and that's perfectly OK.

Chapter Three

HOW TO USE THE LAW OF ATTRACTION EFFECTIVELY

YOU ARE CREATING YOUR FUTURE with every thought you have. But, are you using the Law of Attraction effectively? If your spirit and mind are clouded with negative emotions and ideas, the Law of Attraction can't grant you all of its best blessings.

The Law of Attraction is always working, even when you are upset, unfocused, and full of negative energy. To use the Law of Attraction effectively, you need to calm your mind and stop all self-limiting thoughts. Your spirit needs full belief in your worthiness and path.

Your vibrational energy, or sending out positive or negative emotions, needs to match your desires to create a good intention. Because the Law of Attraction brings like to like, your vibrational energy will affect your blessings, whether good or bad.

Using the Law of Attraction effectively requires that you:
1. Clear your mind
2. Ask for what you want, not what you don't want (for example instead of asking "I don't want to date short men/women" ask instead "I choose to date tall men/women")
3. Believe and act

1. CLEARING YOUR MIND

Self-limiting thoughts seep into your mind consciously and unconsciously. At your lowest, you may think you don't deserve the Universe's blessings. Even when you feel you are prepared to accept a gift, your unconscious mind may sabotage your success by quietly telling you that you aren't worthy or that your blessing won't be enough. To stop these self-limiting thoughts, you need to clear your mind before making an intention.

Meditation is an excellent way to clear your mind. Create a quiet, sacred space where you can relax and focus. Look inside yourself and acknowledge that you have negative thoughts. Let your negative thoughts exist, then move past them and make room for the positive thoughts of total abundance.

Meditation helps you focus your thoughts on the positive aspects of what the Universe holds and your place in it. It clears away negative and self-limiting beliefs and prepares you to open your spirit.

2. ASK FOR WHAT YOU WANT, NOT WHAT YOU DON'T WANT

When your mind is calm and clear, you can now turn to your spirit for direction. What are your deepest desires? What do you need the Universe to gift you? Because the Law of Attraction brings like to like, your spirit needs to be open and honest to bring you fulfillment.

As an example, consider that you are manifesting your desire for a raise at work. If self-limiting thoughts cloud your mind, your spirit won't be open to your fulfillment. When you visualize a larger paycheck, your blessing will not be complete if you also imagine your fears.

Fear of becoming selfish or arrogant when you have more money, fear that you will have to work too hard for your raise, or fear of your raise not being enough will taint your request and limit your blessing. The Law of Attraction doesn't stop only with positive desires. If your request is full of negative factors, the Law of Attraction will bring those too.

3. BELIEVE AND ACT

Manifestation embodies your desires. If you don't believe you have a blessing, the Law of Attraction will not bring your desires to you. Worrying that your request won't be fulfilled, being impatient for the Universe to help you, and fearing that your needs are too high brings only limited blessings.

If you don't believe in your power, you will not effectively use the Law of Attraction to grant your true desires.

The Law of Attraction doesn't reflect only belief. It also brings like to action. Now that you have made your intention and manifested it to the Universe, how will you behave? If you act like your blessing isn't yours, the Law of Attraction can't bring it to you.

Live your life knowing the blessing you desire is already

yours. Treat yourself and other people the way you would if you were blessed, because you are. Don't hide your intention with thoughts of "tomorrow, someday, or maybe in the future." Act now to receive the full benefit of your fulfilled desires.

The Law of Attraction will bring whatever you manifest into reality. Effectively using the Law of Attraction requires that you have a clear and calm mind and an open spirit to ask for what you truly want. When you release your intention to the Universe, believe in your blessing and act accordingly. Effective use of the Law of Attraction allows the Universe to grant your deepest desires.

Chapter Four
HOW TO USE THE LAW OF ATTRACTION FOR SPECIFIC GOALS

ATTRACT MONEY AND FINANCIAL SUCCESS

If you would like to grow your wealth, then spend more time thinking about money!

Read books and watch videos on how to increase your prosperity and make more money. Envision the exact amount you would like and by when. Simply believe it will happen, and it very much will.

Above all, remember to be thankful for everything you already have and appreciate the abundance of all that's good in your life. This will help you create a vibrational match for the financial status that you want in your future.

LOVE AND RELATIONSHIP ATTRACTION

People who can harness the power of the Law of Attraction frequently use it to attract more love and romance into their lives. If you want to attract love into your life, be the love you want to attract!

Be loving and generous with others and yourself. Be grateful for the love you do have in your life and look for ways to express it. The more you create a vibration of love, the stronger the signal you will send to the Universe and gain more power to attract love into your life.

IMPROVE YOUR WELL-BEING

You can also use this universal law to improve your mental and physical health.

Learning to use the Law of Attraction effectively requires becoming a more positive person who focuses on feeling soul-enriching emotions such as gratitude, connection, and abundance.

This allows you to cultivate a healthier mindset, which will inspire you to feel more confident and be inspired to take better care of your physical health.

I DON'T CHASE, I ATTRACT

PRACTICE ATTRACTING YOUR GOALS

According to the Law of Attraction, you create your reality. What you focus on is what you draw into your life. It suggests that what you believe will happen in your life is what does happen.

Some things that you can do to incorporate the Law of Attraction into your own life include:

- Be grateful – I personally start every day by saying "Thank You" three times
- Visualize your goals with as much detail as possible
- Look for the positives in a situation
- Learn how to identify negative thinking
- Use positive affirmations
- Reframe adverse events in a more positive way

While the Law of Attraction may not be an immediate solution for all of life's challenges, it can help you learn to cultivate a more optimistic outlook on life. It may also help you stay motivated to continue working toward your goals.

Chapter Five

THE IMPACT OF THE LAW OF ATTRACTION

THE LAW OF ATTRACTION can produce many positive changes in a person's life. Some reasons why people may experience benefits from it include:

SPIRITUAL EFFECT

The Law of Attraction produces results because it taps into people's spirituality. Spirituality is connected to various health benefits, including reduced stress, better health, lower depression, and better overall well-being.

Many people believe that the Law of Attraction works by aligning God or the Universe with our wishes. This notion suggests that people are all made of energy, and this energy operates at different frequencies. Because of this, it is essential to change the frequency of significance with positive thoughts, especially gratitude for what we already have.

By using grateful, positive thoughts and feelings and focusing on our dreams rather than our frustrations, we can change the frequency of our energy, and the Law of Attraction brings positive things into our lives. What we attract depends on where and how we focus our attention, but we must believe that it's already ours or soon will be.

BETTER WELL-BEING

Utilizing the Law of Attraction may also bring about positive impacts on mental well-being. By focusing on attaining a new reality and believing it is possible, we take more risks, notice more opportunities, and open ourselves to new possibilities. Conversely, when we don't think that something is in the realm of possibilities for us, we tend to let opportunities pass by unnoticed.

When we believe we don't deserve good things, we behave in ways that sabotage our chances of happiness. By changing our self-talk and feelings about life, we reverse the negative patterns in our lives and create more positive, productive, and healthy ones. One good thing leads to another, and life's direction can shift from a downward spiral to an upward ascent.

Research on optimism shows that optimists enjoy better health, greater happiness, and more success in life. They possess traits that allow them to focus their thoughts on their successes and mentally minimize their failures.

One of the foundations of many types of therapy is that changing your self-talk can change your life in a positive direction. A widely used and effective treatment for many conditions, cognitive-behavioral therapy identifies and changes automatic negative thoughts that can produce positive effects and help people achieve better mental well-being.

Chapter Six

TIPS TO MAKE THE LAW OF ATTRACTION WORK FOR YOU

THESE ARE SOME EXERCISES and ideas that can help put the Law of Attraction into practice in your own life.

JOURNALING

Writing down your thoughts can help you better recognize your habitual thought patterns to see whether you tend toward optimism or pessimism and learn more about changing negative ways of thinking. My suggestion is to set a regular time every day to do your journaling, and the best time is at night before you go to bed.

MAKE A MOOD BOARD

Create a visual reminder that helps you maintain a positive mindset, stay motivated, and focus on your goals. You can make a traditional mood board using cuttings from magazines stuck on a large sheet of paper, or you can go the digital way. I use an online design tool to create mine.

PRACTICE ACCEPTANCE

Instead of focusing on what is wrong about the present or what needs to be changed, work on accepting things as they are. This doesn't mean that you won't continue to work toward a better future; it just means that you won't get bogged down by wishing for things to be different right now.

PRACTICE POSITIVE SELF-TALK

If you struggle with being overly self-critical, set a goal to engage in positive self-talk each day. Over time, this may come much more quickly, and you may find that it is harder to maintain a negative mindset. I do my self-talk every morning while putting on my make-up!

The optimistic viewpoint drives proactive behaviors

that, in turn, bring optimists great results in their lives. Optimists don't receive their benefits from their attitudes alone—it's the behavior the attitudes inspire that creates real change.

We can't always control our circumstances, but we can control our responses to them. In this sense, the Law of Attraction can provide the optimism and proactive attitude associated with resilience in difficult situations.

MEDITATE

Meditation is an excellent practice to activate the Law of Attraction and cultivate a clear, positive mind.

Try this simple meditation practice to energize awareness:

- Find a quiet place, close your eyes, and focus on slowing down your breathing.
- Repeat an uplifting word or phrase.
- Move into a state of quiet.
- Imagine yourself surrounded by a sphere of light.

If you are new to the practice of meditation, your thoughts will drift, and your mind will wander at first. Remember not to be hard on yourself when this happens.

This is just part of learning how to meditate.

The point isn't to control your thoughts or try to empty your head of ideas (both of which are impossible.) It's simply to become more aware of your thoughts. Let them go and bring your mind back to the present once you notice yourself thinking negatively.

Consistent meditation practice will help clear your mind of distractions, cleanse your thoughts and enhance your spiritual connection with the Universe. This will naturally help you be a more positive person and attract more good into your life.

Chapter Seven

USING THE LAW OF ATTRACTION TO CREATE A STRESS-FREE LIFE

THERE ARE DIFFERENT THEORIES about how the Law of Attraction works and some important caveats. In this section I share some exercises you can try to use to relieve stress and at the same time manifest the things you want in life.

As we've seen, the Law of Attraction is the idea that our thoughts and feelings create our experiences. What we focus our attention on will be brought into our lives. While the Law of Attraction has an ancient history, its popularity soared in recent years because of books like "The Secret."

According to the Law of Attraction, your thoughts have the power to manifest what you want in your life. For example, suppose you think positively and visualize yourself with enough money to live comfortably. In that case, you will attract opportunities that can make these desires a reality.

On the other hand, if you constantly focus on the aspects of your life that you are unhappy with, you will continue to attract adverse outcomes and experiences.

EXERCISES TO USE THE LAW OF ATTRACTION IN YOUR FAVOR

The Law of Attraction is widely regarded by many as pseudoscience. However, it has also been recognized that it uses several psychological techniques, such as cognitive reframing and visualization, that help people think differently about their circumstances.

If you want to think differently about your life and create a positive environment where change can thrive, here are some exercises to try.

While you can do each one on its own, you might find it helpful to think of each exercise as a step that builds on the work you did in the previous one.

I DON'T CHASE, I ATTRACT

LIST YOUR FRUSTRATIONS

Make a list of all the things in your life that have you feeling frustrated or that you'd like to change—for example, a stressful job, your children's behavior, or conflict in your relationships.

THINK OF THE POSITIVES

Next, start writing. For each frustration on your list, think of every possible positive aspect of the situation. For example, the benefits of your challenging job might be steady income, creative opportunities, or personal growth.

You could then see your job as a vehicle for expanding your level of patience. If not, you might find that the job's purpose is to bring you valuable information about what is not working in your life.

It might be that the positive outcome of the negative experience you're having at your job is that you leave it to pursue a career that is better suited to your talents and skills.

VISUALIZE YOUR WISHES

Once you've listed the things you don't want in your life, write down what you would like to have. Your list isn't just for putting the positive energy out into the world you want to get back; it will also help clarify your goals.

If you're more of a visual thinker than a scribe, you could draw, make a collage, or use a website like Pinterest to curate images of the things you want.

Building and maintaining a visual image of what you want in your life (instead of focusing on what you don't wish to) can be a powerful way to attract positive change and opportunity.

Make a detailed list of what you would like to be different about your life. Each day, take a moment to visualize what your life would look like and how it would feel.

You can also practice "manifesting" what you want. It could be something as simple as finding a parking spot or having a particular flower for your garden. Take time to create a vivid image in your mind of what the flower would look like in your yard, how it would smell, and how it would feel in your hands gathered up in a bouquet.

MAINTAIN A POSITIVE ATTITUDE

Having a positive attitude is about more than putting a

smile on your face; it means working on feeling grateful for what you already have and for what you believe will come. Shift your focus from what you think you lack toward feelings of gratitude and abundance.

You can also strengthen your positive mindset by sharing your goals, dreams, and intentions with others. Spreading your positivity to your loved ones also allows you to get and give support.

THINK, FEEL, ACT

Try to keep your thoughts, feelings, and behavior focused on your goals rather than your frustrations. You can do this by using positive self-talk, visualizing the life you want each day, working on your action plan, spreading kindness, and doing good deeds.

READ QUOTES ABOUT POSITIVE THINKING

Reading positive mindset quotes and quotes about positive thinking can help you get a better sense of what it's like, inspiring you to change. Here are some of the best – you may want to come back to these when we discuss making affirmations below.

If you don't like something, change it. If you can't change it, change the way you think about it.
~ Mary Englebreit

The positive thinker sees the invisible, feels the intangible, and achieves the impossible.
~ Winston Churchill

If you wouldn't say it to a friend, don't say it to yourself.
~ Jane Travis

MORE TIPS FOR HARNESSING THE BENEFITS OF THE LAW OF ATTRACTION

ACCEPT WHAT IS

Avoid focusing only on what you dislike about your life or spending all your time wishing things were different. Accepting what is right now doesn't mean you won't be working on making positive changes—it's more of a reminder not to fall into the trap of constant negativity.

I DON'T CHASE, I ATTRACT

CONSIDER HOW YOU THINK

If you're not sure how your thoughts affect your life, assessing your thought patterns and determining where you are on the spectrum of optimism and pessimism can be helpful.

KEEP A GRATITUDE NOTEBOOK

Record all the things in your life that you're grateful for. There are many benefits to doing this. This practice helps you develop an attitude of gratitude which creates space for more abundance.

REFRAME YOUR FOCUS

Frame your thoughts the same way you would create positive affirmations: Focus on what you want rather than what frustrates you.

Chapter Eight
THE POWER OF POSITIVE THINKING

THE POWER OF POSITIVE THINKING is one of the primary habits of successful people. When you practice positive thinking, you become better at setting the right goals and achieving them. The benefits don't stop there – positivity boosts your mental and physical health, changing how you interact with others.

However, it can be tricky to change entrenched negative thinking patterns even if you know all this. Becoming a positive person can seem challenging – perhaps you've wondered if you're just immune to the power of positive thinking.

In the next chapter I share seven mindful habits proven to create positive thoughts with concrete techniques to practice, including developing new habits that last. As a result, you will begin to see a difference in your everyday life.

POSITIVE VIBES ONLY

Before we go any further, it's important to note that this guide is a positive vibes-only zone. We won't be dwelling on the difficulties of your past, on the things that have held you back, or on the words of that inner critical voice that brings you down.

Instead, we'll be looking at the issue of the power of positive thinking in a productive, constructive, and proactive way.

Perhaps you're reading this and feeling skeptical. However, if you follow this lead, you'll soon start to see that maintaining positive vibes isn't as difficult as it might sound. With some effort, determination, and practice, you can create mindful attitudes that all but eliminate negativity from your life.

I DON'T CHASE, I ATTRACT

If you feel you're not the most positive of people, this can change. Once you tap into your power of positive thinking, you'll be surprised by just how many other things start to change in and around you.

As the Law of Attraction tells us, like attracts like. This means that the more positive you are, the more you pull positive people, opportunities, and choices into your orbit. You begin to vibrate on a frequency of abundance. The abundance in your life only makes you feel more optimistic. Conceptualized in this way, there's no limit to how happy you can be or how much better you can attract.

So, to emphasize again, it's positive vibes only from here on in. Now, let's move on to explore some concrete facts about how consistent, sustained positivity can enhance your life in tangible ways.

7 THINGS THAT HAPPEN WHEN YOU THINK POSITIVE

1. You cope with stress faster and more effectively – instead of dwelling on the negative, positive people look for solutions. And when we find solutions, pressure starts to dissipate.

2. Your health improves – there's evidence that positive thoughts boost disease resistance and enhance the ability to recover from health setbacks.
3. Your relationships with people improve – we're all drawn to positive people, so being positive brings more people into our lives. With a positive attitude, we're also better at communication and negotiation.
4. You become more focused – with the power of positive thinking, you're driven to achieve the things that matter to you. You can tune out the noise and 'tune in' to what needs to be done.
5. You feel more confidence – positivity extends to your view of yourself and your value, boosting your self-worth. The more positive you are, the more you believe in your potential and give yourself opportunities to fulfill it.
6. You become more successful – as a positive person, you not only attract success through the Law of Attraction but are also better at networking and inspiring others.
7. You experience more happiness – it stands to reason that being positive brings you joy, optimism, and satisfaction. When you have a positive mindset, you

I DON'T CHASE, I ATTRACT

notice and appreciate the beautiful things in life.

Chapter Nine

7 MINDFUL HABITS FOR CREATING POSITIVE THOUGHTS

NOW THAT YOU'VE BUILT a deeper understanding of why and how thinking positive can completely transform your life, it's time to delve into how you can become a more positive person.

Yes, most of us can talk ourselves into a positive thought or feeling. Still, it is far-reaching, sustained change that makes the difference. This means it's essential to focus on how to stay positive in all areas of your life.

The following seven habits are proven to help you tap into your power of positive thinking, and I'll explain how you can develop these habits for yourself, starting today. Throughout, I'll offer techniques and suggestions that will help you see the many different ways you might begin to behave differently.

Each of the seven habits can be realized through a range of approaches, and it's important to find those that fit your unique goals, values, and personality.

1. THE POWER OF THE PEOPLE YOU SURROUND YOURSELF WITH

While we can influence others to change, they can also affect us. The phrase "the people you surround yourself with, you become" nicely captures just how vital our social circle can be. So, to become more positive (and stay that way), focus on building connections with people who are good at sending positive vibes.

If you ever ask yourself, "How can I surround myself with successful people?" know that the first step is to nurture your existing relationships with people who are good at achieving their goals. They may have different passions and work in other fields, but if they are positive and successful, you can become more like them just by being around them.

Once again, like attracts like. The more time you spend

with successful people, the more you'll find yourself meeting new people who inspire and motivate you to succeed. This will enhance your power of positive thinking tremendously!

In addition, try to think about success in a broad way. While you can undoubtedly benefit from surrounding yourself with people with fulfilling jobs and excellent salaries, it's easier to stay positive if you look beyond the workplace. For example, you should also surround yourself with people who have thriving love lives and devote time to personal growth.

One of the easiest ways to work out who you want to surround yourself with – and therefore who you want to become – is to do an exercise where you think about your ideal role model. What traits do they have? What are they good at, and how do they act? This gives you a definite sense of the types of people you should spend more time with to develop and sustain a positive mindset.

2. THE POWER OF WORDS

The words you choose also play a dramatic role in being positive. Your language affects your view of yourself, your capabilities, and your expectations. Success habits require you to be realistic yet confident, pushing you to be the best you can be. Consequently, people who attract success learn how to refine their language, stripping it of negativity. But what are the most effective ways to tap into the power of words?

Firstly, make a habit of paying more attention to your word choice. For example, you might set a particular period (e.g., a couple of hours or a day) and then make some notes about which words made you feel empowered and positive.

In contrast, When you notice ways of speaking that don't help you build on positivity, think about how you can change things up. Look to replace words like "can't," "never," and "shouldn't" with aspirational words that describe the life you want to create.

Secondly, designing and reciting affirmations is a powerful way to use words in service of positivity. If you have any doubts, just check out in social media the power of the affirmation that gave the title to this book:

"I don't chase; I attract. What belongs to me will simply find me."

Affirmations are just statements that you say to yourself to support your goals. You can use ones that directly discuss

I DON'T CHASE, I ATTRACT

positivity, like the following:

"I become more positive each day."

"I am happy, confident, and see the best in others."

"I am positive, and I attract positivity into my life."

You can also use affirmations that implicitly reinforce your power of positive thinking towards specific goals in your life.

For example:

"I have all the qualities I need to be incredibly successful"

"Every day, I move closer to the job of my dreams."

"I attract love into my life and give it back to the world."

There are dozens of ways to write affirmations. What matters is that they make you feel good and that they capture what you want to achieve.

3. THE POWER OF CONTRIBUTION

The next major contributor to maintaining a positive mindset revolves around the idea of contribution. The Law of Attraction is magnetic, and so what you put out is what you get back. If you look at how you can make the world a happier place, the Universe will ensure that your generosity and compassion make their way back to you as well.

Plus, combined with the power of positive thinking, studies on the power of kindness show that when we're kind, we end up feeling happier and our stress levels lower. This has a direct and immediate impact on our ability to think positively.

To access the power of contribution, start by asking yourself how you're currently contributing to the world. Try to think of at least five things you're doing for others, and consider which are more effective. Next, try to generate at least five different ideas for ways in which you might give more to others.

There are dozens of things you can do to contribute. Some of which are personal and others which promote happiness in strangers. To contribute to people already in your life, think about chores you might be able to do in times of hardship. You can even take care to listen to people's problems without judging or trying to offer quick fixes.

And you can start with something simple. I decided one day that one of my contributions would be to make people around me smile more. I invite you to try it for one day: just smile. Smile to your loved ones, but also to strangers. You will notice that most people will smile back, and you will love how you feel about having that positive impact on others.

Also, never underestimate how much it can mean just to check in with someone or help them out with something.

And when it comes to other ways of contributing to the lives of strangers, volunteer work is an obvious and effective way to generate positivity by giving back to the world. This might involve working in a shelter for a few hours a week or joining a helpline. When time constraints make this problematic, giving to charity also boosts the amount of positivity in your life and the wider world.

4. THE POWER OF READING

Many of us grow out of reading once we get out of studying, but if you want to create a positive mindset, finding time to read can help. As well as boosting mind power by improving your vocabulary and building your knowledge, reading can create psychological growth in several ways.

For one thing, there are fascinating studies that show how reading can help us become more compassionate and empathetic. When we read, we often have to switch our perspectives. The better we do this, the more we relate to others even dramatically different from us.

There are even brain scans suggesting that when we read fiction in which characters go through specific experiences our brain's activity is similar to actual experiences in real life.

Does empathy really affect our power of positive thinking? There are many different connections between enhanced empathy and keeping a positive mindset. Firstly, if we're more empathetic, we're better at building good relationships involving mutual support.

Secondly, empathy helps us develop a generally sympathetic worldview. Rather than seeing people's behaviors as good or bad, we see them as products of their environments and experiences.

Setting empathy aside, reading holds immense power because it exposes you to new ideas. Reading prompts you to challenge things you may otherwise have taken for granted. This helps you reexamine and replace old beliefs that no longer serve you and inspire you to change.

Finally, reading other people's success stories shows you

how to be successful and reminds you that anything is possible. Try reading a short success story each week for a month, and notice the changes in your mindset.

5. THE POWER OF CHOICE

When you're developing habits that encourage you to focus on the positive, it's vital to remember that you have total control over whether you succeed or not. For example, some people occupy a "victim mindset," telling themselves that they merely respond to circumstances and don't choose what happens to them.

In contrast, if you choose a "creator mindset," you view yourself as the architect of your own life. You get to choose what it looks like and what you attract into it.

Successful people sometimes talk about a "growth mindset," which means adopting the view that you want to evolve and improve. This requires moving away from your comfort zone and moving to a place that feels good in the short term but stifles you in the longer term. Growth can be scary and exciting, as well as give you a sense of becoming who you're meant to be.

When combining the creator mindset with the growth mindset, you get an approach to life that fosters consistent positivity. We all encounter negative or challenging situations, but we can choose to take an optimistic viewpoint. We can choose to look for valuable lessons and opportunities for development.

At first, this may require conscious effort. For example, you might try generating a mind map with the problem in the center and positive ideas surrounding it. If you do this often enough, it will become second nature to read challenges in a positive way, and you'll do it much more quickly.

As a bonus, when you tap into the power of choice and pick optimism over pessimism, you will soon notice that your stress levels massively decrease. Studies suggest that those who take this approach heal more quickly and have better overall health.

6. THE POWER OF EXPERIENCE

Gratitude is a powerful emotion. Any habits that cultivate it also help create a positive mind. When you think of gratitude, you might immediately focus on the most significant achievements and positive experiences in your life – for example, promotions, earning new qualifications, weddings, and births.

I DON'T CHASE, I ATTRACT

Often, we take much of our lives for granted, overlooking the fact that there are many reasons for gratitude. However, when we harness the power of experience with the power of positive thinking, we begin to see the incredible things that happen every day.

I cannot emphasize enough how a gratitude journal is one of the most effective ways to make the most of the power of experience.

Get yourself a notebook or create a document. Enter sources of positivity daily and reflect on feeling grateful for these things.

The aim is to focus on the positive every day. Rather than just focus on the big things, you'll notice that most of your days are ultimately very positive. For example, you might include something beautiful that you saw, a moment of kindness that you experienced, something that made you laugh, or some precious time you took to relax.

When working with a positive mindset, it's also crucial that you make room to be grateful for yourself.

So, when you write in your gratitude journal, challenge yourself to include at least one entry that's just about you.

This might be something big that you have done, felt, or contributed. On other days, you might just be grateful for your health or for a feature or skill that helps you feel confident.

The key idea here is just to develop another habit that encourages self-directed positivity.

Your power of positive thinking will run up a level when you make this a daily habit.

7. THE POWER OF TUNING IN

Finally, tuning in to your higher consciousness can make a massive difference in your ability to create positive thoughts.

What this means is just getting to know yourself on a deeper level. You can practice techniques that tap into your subconscious mind as well as your conscious mind.

Some of the best positive thinking exercises focus on meditation and mindfulness, and I already shared a meditation exercise that can help you get started with this practice.

Even basic breathing exercises can induce calmness and receptivity.

For example, you might set aside ten minutes and try to focus on taking a deep breath in through your nose counting from 1 to 8 and making your belly expand, then count until 4 and exhale through your mouth counting from 1 to 8; then count until 4 and repeat at least 3 times. This helps to settle the mind and get rid of extraneous thoughts that are clouding your thinking. It is natural to get distracted during an exercise like this, but try to let any random thoughts drift away rather than giving them much attention.

When you get used to meditation, you can try different techniques. Another one that you can try involves imagining yourself gradually filling with a golden light.

Feel it start at your toes and work to the top of your head, warming you as it goes. Some people see it as a molten liquid, and others as simply a golden glow. When you open your eyes, you should feel optimistic, energized, and positive.

On days when positive thinking is more complex, you can also try a reverse technique to banish negativity, picturing it leaving your body in the form of a dark cloud. This technique is best followed by the one above, which will help you replace negativity with positivity.

With all of this now planted in your mind, you now can tap into the power of positive thinking to drastically enhance your life.

Chapter Ten
MANIFESTATION AND THE LAW OF ATTRACTION

WE AGREE NOW THAT THE Law of Attraction is that like attracts like. Manifestation is the doing of that. It's almost as if one is a noun and the other one is a verb.

The Law of Attraction works regardless of whether you harness its power or not. Your thoughts attract your circumstances in life. We could debate that from now till we're blue, but that's just what is.

Manifestation is you knowing that your thoughts attract things and harnessing that power purposefully. To manifest is to create using your thoughts, feelings, and beliefs.

To create what? Anything you desire.

If you want to succeed and live your dreams, you can use the Law of Attraction to help manifest your desires.

THE SCIENCE BEHIND THE LAW OF ATTRACTION AND MANIFESTATION

The Law of Attraction and manifestation is not some feel-good, new-age theory. It's science.

The study of quantum physics shows us that everything in the Universe is energy at its basic level. I'm sure you already know that, but let's think about what that means.

All energy vibrates at a specific frequency; lower frequency vibrations are denser. Things that vibrate at that level can be seen by the human eye – such as plants, rocks, your dining room table, and your cat. Things that vibrate at a higher and faster level cannot be seen, for example, thoughts, smells, and sounds.

There is no judgment about this. lower frequency vibrations are not "bad," and higher energy vibrations are not "good." They are just different.

The exciting thing about these frequencies is they are

designed to "seek out" similar frequencies. Hence the Law of Attraction. Like attracts like and manifests it in your reality.

What this means, of course, is that if you're emitting a specific frequency, you attract things of a similar frequency, whether that's people, things, situations, or conditions like wealth or poverty, abundance or lack, health or disease.

And when that happens, they appear in your life.

But there's something else – you will also be attracted to things that resonate with how you're feeling, so it basically works both ways.

Think about it. When you're feeling fed up and miserable, how much do you want to spend time with someone upbeat and happy? Not much. But if your neighbor pops their head over the fence and starts moaning about something bad that's happened to him, you feel a sense of solidarity and enter into the conversation willingly.

However, if you were feeling happy and light-hearted, would you be so keen to engage in that conversation with him? Probably not. It just would not be attractive to you.

So the Law of Attraction is not something you have to do work for you, do certain things at certain times of day, or be a good person or a worthy person or anything in particular. It is simply that you will only attract stuff in tune with your vibration into your reality.

WHAT DOES 'MANIFESTATION' MEAN?

There are many definitions of the word *manifest*. Still, the simplest would be that a manifestation is "something that is put into your physical reality through thought, feelings, and beliefs."

This means that whatever you focus on is what you are bringing into your reality. You may concentrate and manifest through meditation, visualization, or just via your conscious or subconscious.

This process is called manifesting!

For example, if you have been thinking about getting a new job and you focused on exactly what you wanted and when you wanted it, your thoughts and feelings would be strong surrounding this. You could then try to meditate or visualize your goal, which can help manifest it into your reality.

If you then got your new job and it was everything you wanted, you would have successfully manifested it into your life. So, now that you know what manifestation means, it's time to find out how manifestation works.

HOW DOES MANIFESTATION WORK?

As the Law of Attraction, a manifestation is where your thoughts and energy can create your reality. If you are constantly being negative and feeling down, you will attract and manifest negative energy.

The first thing to do when manifesting is to take a good look at your thoughts and feelings. Are you feeling defeated? Do your thoughts surround negativity?

If so, you could begin to manifest things you don't want in your reality. This is why it's essential to clear your mind and have a positive sense when displaying it.

Manifestation doesn't just work with your thoughts; there has to be a form of action on your part. This could be applying for the jobs that suit what you are looking for and going to the interviews.

Trying to visualize your thoughts and feelings about your job will help you feel more positive and motivated to make these changes a reality. This will then push you to take some action and, ultimately, manifest your goals into your life.

HOW DO YOU MANIFEST USING THE LAW OF ATTRACTION?

How do you use the Law of Attraction for manifesting everything you desire? Always remembering that whatever the mind of a man or woman can conceive and believe, it can achieve.

A mind is an incredible tool that has untapped and misused power. Science knows how to go to the moon, yet they only see the tip of the iceberg information about the paranormal and the use of the mind to achieve success, live longer, live better, and be happier.

The term paranormal is a misnomer because there's nothing "beyond normal" using the principles of mind power, such as the Law of Attraction. You use it every day from morning to night. Many people, however, misuse it and attract adverse outcomes.

The Law of Attraction is nothing more than deciding what you want, focusing on visualizing yourself with that, and believing that it already is available. Many untrained men and women use it to achieve either what they want or exactly the opposite.

The mind uses the Law of Attraction without regard for good, bad, like, or dislikes. You get what you ask for, regardless of whether you want it or not.

Suppose you want a house. You draw up the plans, browse magazines and the internet for photos of the different rooms, and picture yourself inside the house greeting guests. One day out of nowhere, you drive past the house of your dreams and find it for sale. You believe this is the right home but have no money to purchase it. Ordinary people would shrug their shoulders and walk away, not you. You know this is the house; you saw it in your dreams and every waking moment. You decide to check with the realtor anyway. Amazingly, the owner wants to finance the house for the seller himself and doesn't need a down payment. The payments suggested fit into your budget. The house is yours. Is it a coincidence? No, it is the Law of Attraction at work.

Do you ever wonder why some people get right up to the door of success only to have it slam in their face? They negatively use the Law of Attraction. They see themselves as failures.

You can create your reality. It works. When you use creative visualization with the Law of Attraction, you direct your mind to see where you want to be. There's nothing mystical about it. It works on several planes. The first is the fact that you are more aware when the opportunity arises. You notice the steps to your goal when they are in front of you. In the example above, you saw the house of your dreams.

The second is that you believe that your dream is attainable. Hence, you take action on it, a move that you would never have attempted without your visualization to confirm that success was possible. In the example above, you stopped and looked at the house, something you usually wouldn't do.

The third may seem mystical and paranormal, but it is just science we don't yet understand. Had someone shown a computer to a person 500 years ago without the present context, he or she would have said it was magic or witchcraft. They would have said that not because it is paranormal but because they didn't yet understand how it worked and all the principals involved in its operation.

I DON'T CHASE, I ATTRACT

That's the same situation we have of the Law of Attraction. Thoughts are things; they are energy waiting to materialize. It requires guidance and focus, but is available to every man and woman. In the example above, your energy influenced the seller's decision to finance the sale, even before you met him. Just like the computer's example, you don't have to understand how it works to use it.

When you learn to use the Law of Attraction in a controlled positive manner, a universe of possibilities begins to show up in your life. It isn't mystical, nor is it magical; you simply don't have the science yet to understand it.

Chapter Nine
HOW TO MANIFEST ANYTHING IN 5 STEPS

WHEN YOU READ ABOUT the Law of Attraction, it can sometimes feel like it will take months or years to manifest anything you desire.

However, if you carefully work your way through the following manifestation steps, it's possible to get results a lot more quickly. If you wonder how to manifest anything in simply 24 hours, you only need five steps.

So, if you follow this straightforward manifestation guide, you may well get exactly what you want in 24 hours or even less!

MANIFESTATION STEP #1: CHOOSE WHAT YOU WANT TO MANIFEST

When you decide on something specific to manifest, you must know precisely why you want this particular thing in your life. And when you're trying to manifest something in just 24 hours, you also have to pick something you believe you can manifest in a day.

So, for example, there's little point in saying you want to start a new business in 24 hours unless you believe you can attain this goal the next day.

However, you may well believe that you can successfully manifest the next step in your journey to a new business in a day, in which case you might set that as your goal (e.g., to complete a business plan, get a loan you need, or find someone to collaborate with.)

When picking a thing to manifest, ask yourself the following questions:

- Do I want this with all my heart?
- How will I benefit from having this?
- When I think about having this, does it feel right?

I DON'T CHASE, I ATTRACT

- How will it be good for me and others?

Whatever you want should be for the greater good and something you want in itself, most likely something that's a significant step on the journey towards a greater manifestation goal.

So, in summary: decide what you want, really connect to having it, and believe that you will receive what you ask for.

MANIFESTATION STEP #2:
GET RID OF THINGS THAT STAND IN YOUR WAY

Unfortunately, almost always, there will be something standing in your way to success. This shouldn't scare you; this is just part of the whole manifestation process.

Keep an eye out for these three most common manifestation blockers:

1. NEGATIVE CORE BELIEFS/MINDSET

Suppose you are in the wrong place emotionally. In that case, you need first to get yourself into the right mindset before you can successfully manifest anything.

You can't be focusing on negativity and expect to attract good things into your life. So take some time to practice self-care. Try meditation and different stress-relief techniques

2. TOXIC PEOPLE

When you are working on manifesting your dream, you need to ensure no one holds you back.

People who don't believe in you, criticize you, and complain about everything are blocks that will keep you from doing your best.

Remember: If it doesn't make you happy, you probably don't need it!

3. TIMING

Sometimes you just need to be patient. Everything you want will happen. But it will happen at the right time and for the right reasons.

So if something isn't happening for you right now, it doesn't mean it never will. Keep believing and keep working on your goal.

Sit back and think about how your manifestation process is going at the moment.

I DON'T CHASE, I ATTRACT

Do you feel like you're on the right path, or is something holding you back?

MANIFESTATION STEP #3: VISUALIZE WHAT YOU WANT TO MANIFEST

You already know the basics of visualization and have at least tried to practice those tecniques a few times. On your current manifestation quest, start by going somewhere that's quiet and private, and spend just a minute visualizing the thing you want.

Pour all your energy and concentration into seeing it with your mind's eye, and let all the good feelings about the object or outcome well up inside you

This step works best if you do a multi-sensory visualization; if you can see, hear, smell, touch, and (if relevant) taste the outcome you're looking to create. Make it as accurate as you possibly can, so it's almost like it's yours already.

Add as many details as you can. Don't try to imagine exactly how the thing or outcome becomes yours; instead, focus solely on the result of receiving what you desire.

Don't think about how your desired object or outcome will manifest. Don't try to see it coming to you through any particular person or means. Your focus should be on the result of receiving the thing of your desire.

MANIFESTATION STEP #4: TAKE ACTION TO MANIFEST WHAT YOU WANT

You can spend the rest of your day pretty much living as you normally would; there isn't any particular action you need to take to make manifestation possible (your intentions will determine your success.) Instead, once you've finished steps 1-2 as described above, you are just waiting for what you want to appear.

However, if you feel the urge to do something specific, whether it immediately makes sense or it's more of an intuition-based yearning, then consider following your gut and taking that action. If it feels natural, do it!

If you find that you don't get the outcome you want within 24 hours or less, look back at the first two steps and go back through them.

I DON'T CHASE, I ATTRACT

As we saw earlier, writing down what you want can give the Universe the extra nudge it needs to fuel your manifestation.

There are some common reasons why you might not be manifesting quickly. In particular, consider whether you doubt the process; do you either not believe you'll get what you ask for because you don't think you deserve it, or perhaps you are questioning whether it's really possible to manifest using the Law of Attraction?

Any negative feelings (e.g., anxiety, worry, anger, and doubt) or negative beliefs can inhibit your results.

MANIFESTATION STEP #5: RECOGNIZE AND APPRECIATE

Although this final step might not look that significant at first glance, it can do a lot to shape your manifestation potential in the future.

The critical thought here is first ask for what you want as if you already have it:

"I'm grateful for the job as Executive Assistant at XYZ company."

"I'm grateful for getting a 10% pay raise on my salary."

"I'm grateful for the promotion to Supervisor."

Also, don't forget to appreciate what you have once you achieve your goal entirely. It can be easy to forget that you asked for what you received, so take proactive steps to prevent this.

Go back to what you first thought and felt when you visualized your desired object or outcome. Connect those experiences with the new experience of having what you want.

Consider the tangible proof you have that thoughts are things and that thinking in a certain way can create substantial changes in the world around you.

The more you make this connection and emphasize it, the better you'll be at manifesting in the future; as you'll replace negative, limiting beliefs and doubts with confident, positive thoughts and feelings.

Chapter Twelve
THE FIVE PRINCIPLES OF MANIFESTATION

1. BEING SPECIFIC

The line "Ask, Believe, Receive" is synonymous with the Law of Attraction. Still, over the years, I've worked on other mindset shifts that can increase your energetic pull – by this I mean, how quickly you're able to attract things into your life.

The first of those is by being specific.

When you want to attract something into your life, you need to put your order into the Universe as you would shopping online. You want the black dress, size 14 in the

Tall range. You're very specific about what you would like to order; the same goes for speaking to the Universe.

Let's say we're starting at our manifestation for beginners' journey. You want to start small to build your trust and belief in the Universe. My first conscious manifestation (I've been doing it all my life without realizing it) was manifesting a pink feather. Soon after reading *The Secret* and deciding to give it a go, I received a birthday present with a pink feather stuck alongside the gift. Coincidence or Universe? I don't care.

Perhaps you want to see a yellow car, or a penguin even. It sounds silly but choosing something you wouldn't usually see makes it all the more amazing when you spot it.

If you want to manifest money, specify the number of dollars and cents you'd like. For example, I tried to make $6,000 last month. I asked the Universe for $6,000; I carried through the steps below, kept my vibrations high, took action, and low and behold, by the end of the month, I had booked over $6,000 worth of work.

I knew exactly why I wanted that amount, I had plans for the money, and I was particular in what I was asking for. I didn't say, oh, I'd love to be able to pay my credit card and maybe a little bit more for spending money for my next vacation. I knew exact figures, what I was going to do with that money, and I kindly put in my order.

2. ASK THE UNIVERSE

What do I mean by asking the Universe? Where do you start?

First of all, you ask with respect. This sounds strange, but to me, the Universe is a being, it's energy, it's a she in my eyes, and that's why I ask her, I thank her, and I trust in her. You don't order your food in a restaurant rudely, so please and thank yous are still relevant in my spiritual house.

There are many different ways you can speak to the Universe, but I like to write mine down and talk out loud. For me, it's a form of praying to a higher force, so I'll either speak out loud to her and ask for what I would like, or I'll write a journal entry about what I would like to have, why, and how thankful I am that it's on its way.

Also, I ask as if it's already happened. By asking it in the present tense as if it's already happened, you're signaling to the Universe that you already believe it to be yours, which is a fantastic thing.

How often should you write? Some people say ask one

and let it go. I believe that reinforcing those positive feelings now and again doesn't hurt, so register as little or as often as you'd like. Sometimes doubt can creep in; we're human after all, so when that happens, reinstate those feelings and journal about how excited you are to have whatever you're manifesting in your life.

As I mentioned earlier, another way of asking the Universe is to create a vision board, where you include words and images that evoke how you'll feel when you receive your order. Is it a new car you want to picture, or a holiday for example? Include images of your specific vehicle, or beautiful exotic beaches, people laughing, or the sunset. Vision boards are an enjoyable way to spend an afternoon, especially if you invite fellow-minded friends over and have a vision board and pizza party!

When I'm putting a vision board together (and I like to do this a few times per year), I like to stick to an absolute maximum of three things I'm manifesting. You can do more, but to be completely honest, I prefer to focus on one thing at a time, so I'm not overloading the Universe with orders. You work in a way that feels comfortable and accessible to you.

3. BELIEVE IN THE UNIVERSE

Now we get to the tricky part for many: believing. How do you believe in something you've never experienced before? I don't want to get too spiritual, but it's about changing your mindset to the what-if. The "oh my god, what if this works" and the "what if I do attract the opportunity to buy a new car into my life" – it turns the usual negative connotation linked to "what if" on its head and lets you get excited about all the new possibilities.

Because I have my living proof that manifestation works in all aspects (I manifested my husband a few years ago!), I find it much easier to lay in bed when I'm visualizing and let myself get excited and feel how I will feel when my dreams come faithful—excited, happy, amazed, calm. The list goes on.

A manifestation I want to work on soon is to buy a Tesla Model S. I'm not a car person, but I recently viewed one and instantly fell in love. I'm not ashamed to say I manifest material things as much as I manifest emotional things. And you shouldn't be either. Having more money in my life has enabled me to help so many more people than I could when I was on a basic living wage. But I digress – money mindset and the way people view manifesting material items is for a whole other book; but let it be known that displaying what makes you happy and raises your energetic vibes is never a negative thing.

In short, let yourself feel good. Get excited. Do a happy dance (is that just me?) Start living as if your manifestation has already come true. For example, when I'm driving my car now, I already imagine that I'm in my new car, that the outside of the car I'm driving already looks like a Tesla. It's why I go online and check it out every day because I believe it will be mine, so I'm already starting the process.

4. RECEIVE AND TAKE INSPIRED ACTION

Contrary to what many cynics say ("Well, I want to win the lottery, so where's my money?"), the Universe doesn't just deliver your order straightforwardly. If I'm manifesting money, I don't expect a man to turn up on my doorstep with a briefcase full of cash.

Quite the opposite, I've learned to open my eyes to opportunities that she's put in front of me and to take something called inspired action. An inspired action is when you meet the Universe halfway and take steps towards making your dreams come true – not just sit on your bum and wait for miracles to appear.

I DON'T CHASE, I ATTRACT

For example, last month, when I wanted to manifest a certain amount of money through my teaching, I started to see so many more opportunities than I usually would if I had had my head down working in a less than positive and open mindset.

You might spot something in a Facebook group that can help you, you might receive an email for something half price. I manifested a Dyson vacuum cleaner this way, after putting it at the very top of my wish list I make at the start of every year – two days later, I got an email from eBay saying they had a half-price sale on the Dyson I wanted to buy. Clever marketers are reading my journal or the Universe; I don't care. My rug is now spotless.

If you're starting small, you might have asked the Universe to show a penguin. That doesn't mean you're waiting for a penguin to walk in front of your car. It could be on a t-shirt. It could be a children's toy you spot or on the Instagram photo of a friend who just visited the zoo. But it will show up; the key is not to be focused on the how.

Open yourself up to the possibilities.

5. BE GRATEFUL

You get so excited that you've managed to attract

something this amazing into your life that you want to start all over again and manifest something else without really giving thanks to the Universe.

How do I show how grateful I am? By writing a gratitude list every single night. Now, this isn't just for the enteral positives because we're human, and I'm realistic. We're all going to have bad things that happen in life. But stick with me here.

Spending five minutes every night thinking about ten things that have happened that day that you're grateful for can change your mindset so much. I find writing about that specific day helps massively because if not, you'll find yourself writing the same things repeatedly.

Yesterday's list for me included a thank you text someone sent, a call from a yoga student that I had which made me feel instantly lighter, having a chance to watch a new show on Netflix, having excellent food in the fridge to be able to cook something for dinner, and the list went on.

Take some time and realize how fortunate you are in comparison to others.

Be specific in what you'd like, choose how to ask the Universe, believe that it will happen and enjoy the feeling of getting excited, take inspired action and be open to how

I DON'T CHASE, I ATTRACT

you will receive your opportunities, and finally, and most importantly, be grateful for the great things to come into your life.

Chapter Thirteen
7 LAW OF ATTRACTION TIPS TO MANIFEST SUCCESS

THE ONLY WAY YOU CAN master the Law of Attraction is with regular practice, and knowing some essential Law of Attraction tips can set you on the path to manifesting your actual desires and less what you don't want.

Awareness and learning to use the Law to your advantage is the first step in changing just about any aspect of your life.

That's great news, right? So you've accepted this, and you're ready to start manifesting the life of your dreams. But how do you get the ball rolling when you've never done it before?

The best advice I can give you is actually sharing some of my daily practices with you.

I developed these practices over several years of testing, and these Law of Attraction tips, which summarize everything covered in this book until now, seem to work best for me, and I also hope for you

So here's the list...let's go!

1. DEFINE AND CLARIFY YOUR GOAL

One reason so many people don't accomplish goals is they aren't specific enough. Manifestation works the same way.

Just saying, "I want to make more money," will not be effective, but saying "I want to earn $10,000 per month by July 1, 2022" will.

A couple of ways to boost your manifesting power is to write out what it would feel like to have already accomplished your goal and read it often. But not just read it, close your eyes, and envision that success scenario in as much detail as you can.

As I mentioned before, creating a vision board can be

helpful if you feel inspired by it and take action towards what you want.

2. SET DAILY INTENTIONS

A great day starts with intention. By deciding the most important things I need to do, or setting a daily theme and then visualizing myself progressing through the day to the best of my ability and accomplishing my tasks with ease. I picture my interactions with others and the activities I think I'll be doing. I envision my perfect day. I imagine myself happy and content.

3. ASK FOR ASSISTANCE FROM YOUR HIGHER POWER

Another tecnique that can be used right away in the morning is to ask for universal assistance in creating your perfect day. You can do this by writing down or saying out loud your requests, which could be something like, "please allow my flight to arrive safely" or "please help me be my best self and truly serve others."

4. RECITE POSITIVE AFFIRMATIONS

You can also write out some flashcards or separate

pieces of paper and put a carefully crafted affirmation on each one. I go through my flashcards a couple of times a day and recite each positive pledge over and over for five minutes. An effective claim should only use positive wording and should always be in the present tense. For example, don't say, "I wish to be debt-free." Instead, say, "I live an abundant lifestyle."

5. KEEP A GRATITUDE JOURNAL

Keeping a gratitude journal is an excellent way to keep your vibrations high. As I shared earlier, I do this every night before I go to bed.

I always list five things I was grateful for that day. It doesn't have to be anything huge; it could be as simple as "I'm grateful to have a roof over my head." I also try not to do the same affirmation more than once (at least to the best of my memory.)

This is truly one of my favorite Law of Attraction tips, and it leaves me with a positive, elevated mood as I go to sleep each day. It's also a great way to raise your vibe if you're trying to manifest during tough times.

6. VISUALIZE YOURSELF CONQUERING YOUR GOALS

And this one is by far my favorite Law of Attraction tip. This is similar to setting your daily intentions but different because it visualizes you achieving a specific goal.

When you picture yourself already at your final destination, in great detail, with the people, place, sounds, smells, and things you want around you, you'll start to attract the tools and other resources you need to make that actual goal (and visualization) a reality. And to be effective, don't just think about accomplishing your goal, really feel it. When you imagine it with emotion, is when the real magic starts to happen.

7. IDENTIFY NEGATIVITY AS IT COMES UP

When you're going about your day, negative things are bound to come up; it's just what happens when we live in the real world. It's how we deal with this negativity that counts. When unfavorable situations arise in my life, I take them head-on and deal with them as swiftly and effectively as possible.

Still, I also imagine the opposite feeling or experience and put all my focus on that. So basically, when negativity shows up, acknowledge it, deal with it as much as possible and then find and focus on the good. I know this can be hard, but you really can find something good in just about every situation you can think of.

When I face a negative situation, I ask myself "What for?" instead of "Why?"

The most important thing to remember when test driving any of the tecniques above is to BE CONSISTENT. Keeping a consistent practice keeps your vibrations high. You should start to notice small changes in a relatively short amount of time. I can't give you a timeline as it's different for everyone. What I can guarantee is that inconsistent practices will bring you inconsistent results or no results at all.

Chapter Fourteen
UNDERSTANDING YOUR SUBCONSCIOUS MIND

YOU HAVE A POWERFUL MIND, and you should know how to use it effectively for your good and the good of others. There are two levels of your mind: the conscious mind and the subconscious mind, the rational mind and the irrational mind.

You think with your conscious mind, and whatever you habitually think sinks down into the subconscious mind. The moment the thought sinks into the subconscious, it starts to work and sees that ideas are attracted to you. The subconscious mind is the creative mind and is created by your thoughts. The subconscious mind is like a fertile land.

It does not know what is being sown as a thought in it. Just like a fertile land can grow a weed and an oak tree irrespective of the seed. Similarly, the subconscious will see to it that the output it provides is following your thoughts.

Here you can imagine the power of the relationship between your conscious mind and the subconscious mind. Imagine if you feed only thoughts and images of abundance and prosperity to the subconscious through the conscious. The whole creative process is nothing short of magic and can manifest itself before we know. The only thing required is a positive channeled thought process that will result in the life you want once planted into the subconscious.

The main point to remember here is that your subconscious mind once accepts an idea; it begins to execute it flawlessly. It does not care whether the idea is good or bad. It takes both the good and bad ideas at face value and, like a loyal servant, goes about executing them. This fact is both freeing and scary. Suppose you plant a negative idea there by emitting lower frequency vibrations. In that case, your subconscious will bring about fear, anxiety, doubt, and ill-health.

On the other hand, if you feed the idea of positivity along with higher frequency vibration, you will find that all the good things you expected and more will be created.

Now that you know how your conscious mind feeds your subconscious mind with a particular thought frequency and how that thought frequency controls your vibration and the Law of Attraction is set into motion.

With this understanding, you've got the keys to the kingdom. The next step is to decide what do you want?

DEFINING WHAT YOU WANT = YOUR GOALS

To manifest your dream life into reality, you should first know what your dream life looks like. One of the ways is to go after what you want. In other words, you should have goals to hit at and go after. If you can't see anything, how are you going to take aim and shoot?

Therefore, it's imperative to have goals and these are seven steps to help you define them:

1. DECIDE WHAT YOU WANT

Ensure that the plan you are aiming for is something you like and not only what you know you can achieve or think you can achieve. Your goal should both scare and excite you at the same time. Set goals that motivate and challenge you equally. Ask yourself "Why it is essential for me to achieve this particular goal?"

2. WRITE DOWN YOUR GOALS

Writing them down will increase your chances of sticking to them. Carry a goal card with you where you have written down what it is that you want. Describe your goal in specific terms. For example, instead of writing, "I want to make lots of money" try "I am so happy and grateful now that I make $10,000 per month and help my family and society." Be as specific as you can. The universe loves clarity.

3. TELL SOMEONE ABOUT YOUR GOALS

Telling a loved one about your plan can increase the probability of sticking to it. But be careful who you share it with as some people are energy vampires that can distract you from achieving what you want.

4. BREAK DOWN YOUR GOALS

This is important for major objectives. Sometimes a big plan can feel daunting for you. If, for example, you aim to be healthier, you can break your fitness path down to smaller timelines and smaller tasks like for example first jogging in intervals of 5 minutes on and 5 minutes off for 30 minutes, and after one week increasing the frequency to 10 minutes on and 5 minutes off for 40 minutes. Such smaller goals are measurable, actionable, and will help you to reach your bigger goal.

5. DON'T PROCRASTINATE

Start now. Take the first step, and the path will be laid in front of you. You will be amazed to see things 'falling in place,' and all the steps needed will be revealed to you if you move towards your goal with confidence. Just take the first step. Trust me: when you take one step towards your goal, your goal takes two steps towards you.

6. KEEP ON GOING

On your path of achieving your goals, you will find yourself stuck many times. Don't stop as all the hard work you did till now will be wasted. You will be frustrated that the progress is not there as you want, but you have to persevere and have faith in the unseen. Just sit down and explore ways to do things differently. Don't hesitate to ask for help wherever you feel stuck. Remember, if you move confidently toward your goal without giving up, you will find inspiration and success at unusual places and hours. What you are seeking is seeking you too.

7. GIVE THANKS

When you reach your goal, enjoy the moment and thank all who made it possible. Appreciate the journey which you were put through and note down what you learned along the way.

CONCLUSION

While it may sound too good to be true, and can take time to get the hang of, the Law of Attraction is about shifting your mindset to one of abundance, calling in what you want, and aligning your actions with your desires.

When you can do those things, you can become the architect of your life and attract a host of possibilities.

ABOUT THE AUTHOR

VERA WRIGHT is an internationally recognized Master Teacher and Healer. Her work is focused on helping others connect with their inner self, and to find and use their voice to see a much larger picture of life than meets the eye.

She is also a meditation teacher and Kundalini yoga instructor trained in Thailand and India. Vera specializes in various techniques for the Awakening of Consciousness and is founder of two organizations devoted to helping empower those seeking self-determination, purpose, and fulfillment through the power of manifestation.

She lives in California with her husband Bob and their two cats.

Printed in Great Britain
by Amazon